›TOURIST

es

I think the series is wonderful and beneficial for tourists to get information before visiting the city.

-Seckin Zumbul, Izmir Turkey

I am a world traveler who has read many trip guides but this one really made a difference for me. I would call it a heartfelt creation of a local guide expert instead of just a guide.

-Susy, Isla Holbox, Mexico

New to the area like me, this is a must have!

-Joe, Bloomington, USA

This is a good series that gets down to it when looking for things to do at your destination without having to read a novel for just a few ideas.

-Rachel, Monterey, USA

Good information to have to plan my trip to this destination.

-Pennie Farrell, Mexico

Great ideas for a port day.

-Mary Martin USA

Aptly titled, you won't just be a tourist after reading this book. You'll be greater than a tourist!

-Alan Warner, Grand Rapids, USA

Thank you for a fantastic book.

-Don, Philadelphia, USA

Even though I only have three days to spend in San Miguel in an upcoming visit, I will use the author's suggestions to guide some of my time there. An easy read - with chapters named to guide me in directions I want to go.

-Robert Catapano, USA

Great insights from a local perspective! Useful information and a very good value!

-Sarah, USA

This series provides an in-depth experience through the eyes of a local. Reading these series will help you to travel the city in with confidence and it'll make your journey a unique one.

-Andrew Teoh, Ipoh, Malaysia

>TOURIST

GREATER THAN A TOURIST – CHANIA CRETE GREECE

50 Travel Tips from a Local

Dimitra Papagrigoraki

Greater Than a Tourist- Chania Crete Greece Copyright © 2017 by CZYK Publishing LLC. All Rights Reserved.

All rights reserved. No part of this book may be reproduced in any form or by any electronic or mechanical means including information storage and retrieval systems, without permission in writing from the author. The only exception is by a reviewer, who may quote short excerpts in a review.

Cover Template Creator: Lisa Rusczyk Ed. D. using Canva.
Cover Creator: Lisa Rusczyk Ed. D.
Image: https://pixabay.com/en/old-town-old-city-marina-1700592/

Edited by: Melanie Hawthorne

Greater Than a Tourist
Visit our website at www.GreaterThanaTourist.com

Lock Haven, PA

ISBN: 9781980993896

>TOURIST
50 TRAVEL TIPS FROM A LOCAL

>TOURIST

BOOK DESCRIPTION

Are you excited about planning your next trip?

Do you want to try something new?

Would you like some guidance from a local?

If you answered yes to any of these questions, then this Greater Than a Tourist book is for you.

Greater than a Tourist- Chania Crete Greece by Dimitra Papagrigorakis offers the inside scoop on Chania. Although there is nothing wrong with that, as part of the Greater Than a Tourist series, this book will give you travel tips from someone who has lived at your next travel destination.

In these pages, you will discover advice that will help you throughout your stay. This book will not tell you exact addresses or store hours but instead will give you excitement and knowledge from a local that you may not find in other smaller print travel books.

Travel like a local. Slow down, stay in one place, and get to know the people and the culture. By the time you finish this book, you will be eager and prepared to travel to your next destination.

>TOURIST

TABLE OF CONTENTS

BOOK DESCRIPTION
TABLE OF CONTENTS
DEDICATION
ABOUT THE AUTHOR
HOW TO USE THIS BOOK
FROM THE PUBLISHER
OUR STORY
WELCOME TO
> TOURIST
INTRODUCTION
1. Visit The Breath-Taking Village Of Loutro
2. Best Cocktails In Town
3. Wine Tour And Wine Tasting
4. Stargaze In The White Mountains
5. Take A Tour in Pamako Olive Oil Factory
6. Balos – Gramvousa
7. Enjoy a Traditional Dinner
8. Have The Best Dessert And Views In Chania City
9. See The Pink Sand Beach
10. Go Through A Beer Tour
11. Tabakaria
12. Eat Authentic Bougatsa In Iordanis
13. Have Lunch In Anidrous

14. Spend A Day In Palaiochora
15. Stay Up And See Ghosts
16. Drive To Sebronas Village For Lunch
17. Pic-Nic By A Lake
18. Have A Drink In The First Jazz Bar In Crete
19. Enjoy A Day Sailing
20. Bungee Jump From The Second Tallest Bridge In Europe
21. Eat Patsa And Vrasto In The Old Market
22. Be Brave And Try Lamb's Head Like A Local
23. Enjoy Seafood In Don Rosario's Restaurant
24. Visit Kolibari
25. The WW2 Ally Cemetery
26. Visit The Archaeological Museum
27. Holy Trinity And Gouverneto Monasteries
28. Walk Around The Lively Street Of Daliani
29. Visit And Paddle Across The Kourna Lake
30. Have Meze And Listen To Live Cretan music in 'Chalkina' restaurant
31. Stavros Beach (Zorba's Filming Location)
32. A View From The Top (Rosa Nera)
33. Aptera Fortress
34. Take Cretan Dance Lessons
35. Splantzia Square (1821)
36. Visit Milia, a Traditional Village
37. See The Oldest Olive Tree In The World

38. Visit Eleftherios Venizelos' House
39. Have Coffee in 'Kipos' Historic Cafe
40. Horseback In Dere
41. 'Agrotikos Augoustos'
42. Attend a food – drink festival
43. Seitan Limania
44. Dine At Pallas Rooftop
45. Loutraki Beach
46. Bike Through Therisso Gorge
47. Visit the Botanical Park and Gardens
48. Walk to the lighthouse
49. Devour a Sfakiani Pitta
50. Sabbionara views

Top Reasons to Book This Trip

50 THINGS TO KNOW ABOUT PACKING LIGHT FOR TRAVEL

Packing and Planning Tips

NOTES

>TOURIST

DEDICATION

This book is dedicated to my father Michael Papagrigorakis who lived an extraordinary life full of travel, laughter and endless adventure.

\>TOURIST

ABOUT THE AUTHOR

Dimitra Papagrigorakis is a twenty six year old hopeless romantic who enjoys all forms of art; from writing as a new freelancer, to drawing, dancing and cooking.

Gladly Chania being a city she knows well as a local, she can practice all these forms of art to the best of her ability.

Her policy when she meets new people is to make them feel welcome. Her philosophy has been to show those who aren't local, the local way. Something she applies when she ventures herself.

Traveling is her way of life and a learning experience she wants to pass on to everyone she meets.

HOW TO USE THIS BOOK

The Greater Than a Tourist book series was written by someone who has lived in an area for over three months. The goal of this book is to help travelers either dream or experience different locations by providing opinions from a local. The author has made suggestions based on their own experiences. Please do your own research before traveling to the area in case the suggested places are unavailable.

FROM THE PUBLISHER

Traveling can be one of the most important parts of a person's life. The anticipation and memories that you have are some of the best. As a publisher of the Greater Than a Tourist book series, as well as the popular 50 Things to Know book series, we strive to help you learn about new places, spark your imagination, and inspire you. Wherever you are and whatever you do I wish you safe, fun, and inspiring travel.

Lisa Rusczyk Ed. D.
CZYK Publishing

\>TOURIST

OUR STORY

Traveling is a passion of the "Greater than a Tourist" series creator. Lisa studied abroad in college, and for their honeymoon Lisa and her husband toured Europe. During her travels to Malta, an older man tried to give her some advice based on his own experience living on the island since he was a young boy. She was not sure if she should talk to the stranger but was interested in his advice. When traveling to some places she was wary to talk to locals because she was afraid that they weren't being genuine. Through her travels, Lisa learned how much locals had to share with tourists. Lisa created the "Greater Than a Tourist" book series to help connect people with locals. A topic that locals are very passionate about sharing.

>TOURIST

WELCOME TO
> TOURIST

>TOURIST

INTRODUCTION

Chania is a city and county full of surprises, sounds and flavors. When it comes to variety you can have it here in this picturesque place that has combined the Venetian, Greek and occasionally Turkish architecture.

What is most fascinating about the small city of Chania and county it resides in is the combination of traditional and the new; the mountains and the enchanting beaches.

Whether you are a young adult or in retirement, there are always things suitable for all ages. We have got it all; from clubbing, to fine dining and extreme sports.

Crete is a traditional island, you can still see people live the same way they did forty years ago and that is the beauty of this place. We maintain our original character.

My goal here is to take you to the best places I have found as a local, while being friendly and making sure you feel it is worth a visit. Enjoy it and welcome to beautiful Crete.

>TOURIST

1. VISIT THE BREATH-TAKING VILLAGE OF LOUTRO

I cannot emphasize enough the importance of seeing this place. I am a local and yet I visited Loutro just this year (2017). I had previously heard people describing the crystal clear waters, but I never expected to see what I did in my wildest dreams.

It has recently become more popular among tourists, but trust me it is the number one place in Chania to see.

Would you like to visit a traditional white-washed village, with blue windows and turquoise waters you just cannot get out of? Well then, welcome to Loutro where time just stops.

To reach this paradise you can only do so by ferry. The ferry leaves every day from Sfakia (south coast of Chania) three times a day; the first one departing at 10.30 and last one at 18.30. The ferry ride lasts approximately twenty minutes and you get to see the water caves from Sfakia to Loutro.

2. BEST COCKTAILS IN TOWN

In my opinion the best cocktails in town can be found in the newly established restaurant Boheme, in Chalidon street (tucked in an alley). It is known among the locals for its fine dining and most of all, the mouth-watering cocktails.

You should not leave without devouring the Sueno de Suerte cocktail, which was awarded twelfth in the Diplomatico Worldwide tournament made by the talented Lefteris Broupis. It is truly worth the award.

Boheme is distinctive for its rustic yet vintage décor, jazz and occasionally rock and roll music; it is an excellent and innovative combination of yesterday and today.

3. WINE TOUR AND WINE TASTING

For wine tasting, I want to encourage you to visit the Dourakis Winery which is a family-run business.

The winery is one of the first in Chania to operate, opened 1998 by Andreas Dourakis, who studied the art of wine in Germany; a polite man who

>TOURIST

works for the business now as he has done since day one.

All of their of wines are exceptional and high quality, my absolute favorite ones are the Malvazia Aromatica (a white dry local variety), the Kydos a combination of local variety (kotsifali) and the Syrah, known worldwide with for having smooth to the pallet combination that I enjoyed most. Last but not least, I should also mention the dessert wine Euphoria – Romeiko, which was awarded with the seventh place in the National wine competition.

I have been drinking Dourakis wine for a while now, and it comes as no surprise that the wine is only improving with time.

4. STARGAZE IN THE WHITE MOUNTAINS

Are you tired of the busy lifestyle of your hometown and want to quiet the buzz inside your head?

The answer is Kalleri's shelter. Situated at an altitude of 1680m, east of Omalos plateau and just a 5km hike up the dirt road (approximately 1.30 hours).

The shelter can accommodate about 50 people and is very affordable.

You can go anytime from April to October and also during the winter, if you don't mind hiking in thick snow, but make sure to make a reservation. My suggestion is to go in the summer to see everything in clearly. During this time there are also two most extraordinary things to be witnessed. The sunset and then the stars that follow; the sky is so clear you can actually see the Milky Way and nebulas as well.

Alternatively, you can also drive to the top if you rent a 4x4 if you don't want to stay here overnight.

5. TAKE A TOUR IN PAMAKO OLIVE OIL FACTORY

This is nothing new but as you know, Greeks love their olive oil and for good reason. Olive oil is beneficial to us all in the long run. My day job involves cooking, so naturally I try to educate myself on everything it involves. As such, I wanted to tour an olive factory. I heard a local producer of this olive oil is from my home region (selino), so I visited. The company is new yet already successful in the three years its been operating, run by the young and

>TOURIST

innovative Eftihi Androulaki. The oil is produced by traditional methods. Century varieties of olives used include, tsounati (a rare variety) and a much newer type, koroneiki. No chemicals or refined oils are used, gaining it the award of one of the highest phenolic, organic olive oils of the world in 2017. The tour is done in the stunning mountain location of Astrika.

What to expect: A tour of the factory and olive groves, a two hour seminar for a better understanding of olive oil including how to evaluate it, and some olive oil tasting.

6. BALOS - GRAMVOUSA

This wouldn't be a guide of Chania if it didn't include Balo and Gramvousa. Therefore with this tip, I will be less than original but I still encourage you to see this major tourist attraction. Balo is a lagoon located in the west peninsula of Chania. Gramvousa is an uninhabited island with a small shipwreck on its shore.

The water, just like in most parts of Crete, is clear enough to see the gold sand below. The highlight of this excursion though is hiking down the path where you can see the magnificent and dream-

like views of the west edge of the island. The only problem
 if you hike down is that you can't see Gramvousa, because it is too far to swim across.

If you decide you want to see both, you will have to be in Kastelli port early enough to purchase tickets for the ferry that will take you to Gramvousa for an hour and to Balos lagoon.

7. ENJOY A TRADITIONAL DINNER

This restaurant is literally off the beaten track in Ano Stalo, 9 kilometers away from Chania city in the mountains, but worth the drive to find it. I have gone there for dinner after it was suggested by a friend.

I have been back many times and have never been let down. When I think traditional food, I think Leventis, which has earned four golden awards in National competitions.

Originally situated in the building behind it, it housed a stable and a traditional cafe, until eventually the family turned it into a restaurant. Now you can enjoy the mountain views paired with a glass of local of wine.

>TOURIST

The food is all freshly made and prepared by the mother of the brothers who own it, Giorgo and Panagioti. Be sure to try their 'antikristo' lamb, rumored to be the best in Chania.

8. HAVE THE BEST DESSERT AND VIEWS IN CHANIA CITY

From the first day of operation sometime in 1997 Koukouvagia (which translates to 'the owl'), has been a success with locals. Not only because of the view it offers, but also its delicious desserts like chocolate cake and ice cream (Zoumero). It has received the a great reputation for good reason. I don't know a single teenager who has not skipped school in the middle of the day to hitch-hike to Koukouvagia (not that I encourage either), but it is where everyone goes for a cold coffee and a mouth watering dessert.

My absolutely favorite is the 'kantaifi with masticha ice cream'. Once there and if you are a fan of espresso try the 'freddo espresso' or 'freddo cappuccino', a cold version of your usual espresso. It is a Greek invention, not Italian. You can walk to the gardens next to it, Venizelos Graves, and enjoy the panoramic views.

9. SEE THE PINK SAND BEACH

Elafonisi is an island you can literally walk to.

This island is 72.5km from Chania center, a two hour drive. It is an attraction known to tourists now, but due to its pink sand (caused by the tiny shreds of coral) and turquoise contrast, I must insist you visit.

Beware of the prices of sunbeds and ensure you pick up your trash while there. The area is protected highly and was granted the title of most beautiful beach in the Mediterranean.

Furthermore, mind your step as occasionally rare and extinct turtle eggs can be found on the small island's shore.

On the way there, make sure to have a little workout climbing the steps to Chrysoskalitissas church.

>TOURIST

10. GO THROUGH A BEER TOUR

In Zounaki village in the middle of nature, operates our very own Charma micro-brewery, just twenty minutes from the center of Chania.

This newly renovated brewery offers tours to see where the magic happens, and allows visitors to try the beers they produce.

Initially it opened in 2007 with just two beers (Blonde Lager and Dunkel), but now it has expanded and new equipment has allowed them to add Pale ale and Special brews.

This brewery's philosophy is simple: Make good quality, organic beer without added chemicals and respect the environment you work in.

The beer is pure, unfiltered, made with local ingredients and is only found on tap. It is not bottled to ensure that the final result is of top quality.

Travelling.
'It leaves you speechless,
Then turns you
Into
A storyteller.''

-IBN BATTUTA

11. TABAKARIA

Featured in many movies, the most recent being 'Two Faces in January', is the neighborhood Tabakaria. A little port that takes you back in time with its post-war feel and authenticity that survives to this day.

The buildings were once used as leather factories but now have been left tonature and time. This is both good and bad. You can still see the originality here, but there is a sense of loneliness and sadness in the atmosphere. It reminds you that this was a place vivid with laughter, songs, working people and running children.

Be sure to take in the views with a glass of wine at 'Thalassino Ageri' restaurant and good quality food while you're there.

12. EAT AUTHENTIC BOUGATSA IN IORDANIS

One cannot visit the city of Chania without tasting this incredible local specialty.

>TOURIST

Iordanis is a family cafe that has passed on the art of bougatsa making for the past 93 years. Bougatsa comes from the Turkish word, pie. The art of this product, that can never be replaced, arrived in Crete across Jordan, and was sold to a Cretan-Turk during the Turkish hold (1924).

It has been a tradition a long time, and is incredibly popular with most of the locals.

I came to find this dish through my father who would wake me up at the crack of dawn, just to get the first pieces as he believed these were the best.

The cafe or shop (so to speak), is located on Apokoronou Street where it will surely be for generations to come.

13. HAVE LUNCH IN ANIDROUS

For the longest time I hadn't known of this small village until I was told about it by a local palaiochora. This little place is also out of anyone's way at 76km from Chania, and you have to go through a narrow gorge to get to it.

In Anidrous there is only one restaurant the 'scholio', which means 'school', which is also decorated like one; the decor makes you feel like you are having lunch in a school in the 50's.

From the patio you can get lost staring at both the mountains and the Lybian Sea.

As for the food, it may be simple but it is an explosion of flavors to the pallet. It is mainly traditional food, but with their personal spin on it.

Take my word for it: take the car and drive there, you shouldn't leave this island without seeing this place at least once.

14.SPEND A DAY IN PALAIOCHORA

A true gem of combinations is Palaiochora. A place where you can find twenty different beaches to swim, mountains to hike, bars and restaurants for all preferences. There is also a vegetarian restaurant there which is rare for Crete. There are only two that I know of, 'the eye' in Palaiochora and 'plaka' in Chania on Sifaka street – in case you are looking for somewhere to eat without meat.

What I like to do when I'm in Palaiochora though, is drive to Grammeno beach and walk through the Cedrus tree forest. But no matter what I do throughout the day there, one thing is certain, I

>TOURIST

must see the sunset at Jetee beach bar where I park myself on one of the bungalows or hammocks.

A nice addition to this beautiful village is the fortress on the top of the hill. It is named 'Selino' and it has been destroyed and rebuilt at least three times.

15. STAY UP AND SEE GHOSTS

You are probably wondering if I have misspelled this but I have not. Yes, I speak of ghosts. Boo!

Legend has it that on the sunrise of June 1st every year, one can witness the raging ghosts of the warriors who fought in Fragocastello fortress on the south coast of Chania (by Chora Sfakion where you take the ferry to Loutro).

The ghosts are called 'Drosoulites' by the locals which means 'the early comers', because to see them you must be up before the rise of the sun. These ghosts depict the 600 warriors who fought against 10,000 Turks in the battle of Fragocastello May 17th 1828.

A funny fact, when we decided to visit it fell on Memorial Day weekend. Unfortunately, we fell asleep just before sunrise and saw nothing. However our dog was barking at the water, where they are said to be seen; most though swear to the existence of these ghosts.

Why don't you be the judge?

16. DRIVE TO SEBRONAS VILLAGE FOR LUNCH

In Crete when we meet someone we ask them where are you from? What is your village? The answer is not where each of us grew up, but where our father grew up. That is our 'village'. Mine is the Selino region and to be more specific 'Maragiana' (No one will ever know it – it has two residents at the moment). Sebronas is two villages before my own, so this is a route I know well.

Here you are in the real countryside. No shops, no gas stations, nothing; just trees, birds and fresh water all around you. The drive is stunning but the roads are narrow and twisty – oh well! That's Crete.

There in the tiny village is Bobolaki's restaurant, a traditional cafe which is soley operated by a local family. They pick their own greens and bring in their own meat. Everything is fresh and made using traditional recipes and methods.

>TOURIST

17. PIC-NIC BY A LAKE

Agia Lake is a small, man-made lake with great value and geological importance to Chania. There you can find rare kinds of frogs, birds and other smaller water species.

I like to sit further in the gardens where I will not be attacked by bugs, just far enough that I can see the water. There is a great open space next to a small stream, by an abandoned stone house now overcome by nature.

The walk around the lake is magical and a must-see while you're in Crete.

Another suggestion is to see the sunset from the cafe Edesma that overlooks the beautiful lake, it's a rare opportunity and not to be missed.

18. HAVE A DRINK IN THE FIRST JAZZ BAR IN CRETE

In the most picturesque alley of the old harbor 'Odos Aggelon' which translates to the street of angels, is a welcome addition to the beauty of the tiny colorful alleys; 'Fagotto' bar. The first Jazz bar in Crete and possibly in Greece, established in the year 1978.

The interior is decorated with paintings of classic jazz and blues legends, while the building itself is made of stone, giving it a cozy and timeless character.

I like how every time I walk down this alley I can hear the sound of a saxophone, echoing from inside.

Enjoy the sounds of the past selected by Petros the friendly owner, with a classic cocktail made by talented staff.

The bar also holds live jazz and blues events. It is a rare a jewel of the harbor.

19. ENJOY A DAY SAILING

Although I have been a local for the past twenty six years, I do enjoy doing some things locals don't tend to, just to experience it and relax. Once I even rode a horse carriage around town, not because I was too lazy to walk but to see what others see.

I also like having the salty water splash on my face and the sea mess with my hair. So I took the first sailing trip of my life and swore to do it again.

>TOURIST

I chose Notos-sailing, run by the friendly Nikos. In this private excursion you can see Chania from another perspective.

We started from the old harbor at 10.00 am and were back by 17.00. I got to see Machairida, Lazareta, Theodorou and Menies bay as well. The cruise included wine and small snacks.

Give it a shot and explore Chania by water. Find the package that suits your budget and you will not regret it. My only suggestion is to plan it as a group like I did, it's a lot more fun to see the sights with friends old or new.

20. BUNGEE JUMP FROM THE SECOND TALLEST BRIDGE IN EUROPE

Are you a thrill seeker? Tired of swimming in our enchanting waters and want more out of your vacation? I think that means you should experience Crete's extreme sports.

You can also find sky-diving in Chania during the summer months, but I chose to bungee jump instead from the tallest bridge in Greece, and second highest in Europe.

This bridge is 138m high and located in the middle of nowhere, 85km from Chania, in Aradaina-Sfakia. The drive there is remarkable. You can also book a room nearby and take your time looking at the wilds.

What can you really expect from the jump? It is terrifying, you feel you will fall before you do or have a heart-attack throughout the whole experience. It is the best feeling in the world once you stop bouncing though and a pure adrenaline rush

> *''All journeys have*
> *Secret destinations*
> *Of which*
> *The traveller is unaware.''*

-Martin Buber

21. EAT PATSA AND VRASTO IN THE OLD MARKET

I cannot count on one hand the amount of times I have had vrasto and patsa after a very drunken night. This specialty is for those who want to sober up, or not wake up with a hangover.

The first time I had it however, I wasn't drunk. This was one of my father's favorite things to have, along with bougatsa. We would wake up at 05.30am and eat hot fresh soup from the butcher shops in the old market.

My mouth is watering as I am typing this.

Even If you aren't the type to drink and you don't have a hangover, just wake up early and try these two specialties. Life is all about trying new things; even beef soup with intestines.

22. BE BRAVE AND TRY LAMB'S HEAD LIKE A LOCAL

I come from a village and so often I slip into my old eating habits. I apologize if you are a vegetarian or vegan, but generally in Crete meat dishes are all you will find (before I go into more details you should probably skip this tip, If you are). Meat and more meat. We get creative with it too. It is how we have been raised, to eat what is given to us.

Back when my father was young, meat was a luxury. His diet would usually include vegetables, bread and olive oil. When they did have meat, like lamb, they would find ways to A. make it last and B. have more, therefore they wasted nothing.

Growing up in a traditional household full of hungry – loud Cretans, I was made to eat like a boy. Not your usual Greek girl. I much enjoyed eating everything the lamb's head had to offer. That includes the eyes, brain, tongue and cheeks; all but the bone. We cook it in many ways, in the oven with potatoes or orzo, and most commonly on a spit with herbs.

23. ENJOY SEAFOOD IN DON ROSARIO'S RESTAURANT

Do you enjoy a good seafood dish? Crete is not only known for our meat dishes but for our fresh seafood too. You can find good seafood nearly everywhere with the exception of the old harbor (in my personal opinion). But there is one restaurant not known to many tourists and they have the best seafood I have tried to this day.

The owner of the restaurant is Italian and has combined Italian cooking methods with Greek, making a mouth-watering result out of every dish you try.

I most enjoy the clam spaghetti, and the steamed mussels with its discreet garlic finish.

This restaurant is located in Platani, just off the exit of the main highway going towards Rethimno, to the right.

24. VISIT KOLIBARI

Another waterfront village with character and amazing restaurants.

Just thirty minutes away from the center, yet you can feel a different air to the place; like you aren't in Chania anymore.

While there you should:
- Walk to the church of Virgin Mary.
- Have lunch in Argentina restaurant or Nikiforos.
- Enjoy a coffee with view of the waves. The ideal place is the 'On the rocks' a cafe with friendly staff and good drinks.

There is a big celebration on the 14th of August in the area that shouldn't be missed but if you decide to do so, drive carefully on the way back as it is madness on the roads that day.

25. THE WW2 ALLY CEMETERY

A rather gruesome title for a tip here, but I had to include it nevertheless.

This cemetery was built after the WW2 in honor of the fallen soldiers who died to defend our freedom.

The chilling site is found and well cared for in the Vlite area of the Souda municipality.

The bodies buried there were on the allies as the title suggests, and among them are soldiers from the United Kingdom, Australia, New Zealand, India, Canada and even South Africa.

Every year ceremonies are held in their honor.

Why not pay your respects while visiting?

26. VISIT THE ARCHAEOLOGICAL MUSEUM

The archaeological museum is housed and found in Chalidon street, within the walls of the Catholic church of Saint Francis. Before its use as a museum it has been through many changes. It has been a

>TOURIST

warehouse during WW2, a theater and a mosque as well, during the Turkish hold.

The building started operating as a museum in the year of 1963. The interior was restored between 1977-1981 and in the year 2000, a new room was added to display the collection of the nationally known politician 'Mitsotaki'.

27. HOLY TRINITY AND GOUVERNETO MONASTERIES

Just a five minute drive from the airport, you can find a Venetian renaissance influenced monastery. It has stood since the year 1611 when the monk Jeremiah Tsakarolo lived, one of the members of a reputable Venetian-Cretan family. The building itself was used in several ways after its construction. Due to the frequent wars it has witnessed, it took 282 years to complete.

It still maintains a renaissance air to it and you will be overwhelmed by a feeling of peace while on its grounds. You can even ask to try wine and olive oil produced by the monks.

Next go through the lot to the right before leaving the church and slowly drive up the curvy mountain to the monastery of Gouverneto, another historic building. Make sure to cover your legs and torso (it is the monastery's policy), and hike down the path to see the Venetian bridge, ancient village and narrow cave of Saint John. To access the latter you must be well equipped with flashlights and proper boots because it is rather dangerous.

28. WALK AROUND THE LIVELY STREET OF DALIANI

A usually calm place, Daliani has lately become known for new bars and cafes. Here a tower casts shade on the cobble-stone alley, one out of the two minarets left in town.

The alley is busy with chatty young locals and you can find everything there; from street food to greasy pizza to a variety of wines.

The places I like the most are: Karolos monastery also known as 'kibar', where you can find noteworthy cocktails and a good selection of beer. The other favorite of mine is the hole in the wall, 'Miniatoura' (which literally translates to miniature)

>TOURIST

where you can listen to rock music. Just across the street you will find the small restaurant 'papoutsomenos ntakos' which serves good meze at very reasonable prices.

29. VISIT AND PADDLE ACROSS THE KOURNA LAKE

Lake Kourna is the only sweet water natural lake in Crete and located at the borders of Chania county, and Rethimno. The lake is surrounded by beautiful hills and Cretan wildlife.

It is an ideal day trip for families with children, as there is a playground and paddle boats you can use to see the lake. There is the option for coffee or lunch in one the cafes by the water too.

Make sure to not step into the shadows though, or you might be confronted by the lake's beautiful female ghost. She is said to lure men towards the lake and drown them. Just like a Celtic kelpie; only our myth is of a vengeful spirit.

30. HAVE MEZE AND LISTEN TO LIVE CRETAN MUSIC IN 'CHALKINA' RESTAURANT

If you are wondering where the locals go for fun or food, here's the answer. Cretan's enjoy restaurants as much as any other culture but what we prefer is having a meze and listening to live music. Meze is a small dish similar to the Spanish tapas.

Usually diners order five or six small dishes which everyone digs in to, with a carafe of wine or honey raki (rako-melo) to drink.

There are many restaurants like this one around town, but I always choose Chalkina because of their innovative dishes and live shows, usually every night.

There you will be made to feel like a local, and can see the true colors of this wonderful land.

"If we were meant to be in one place,
we'd have roots instead of feet"

-Rachel Wolchin

>TOURIST

31. STAVROS BEACH (ZORBA'S FILMING LOCATION)

We are proud of many things in Chania and one more is the fact that one of the most famous movies of all time, Zorba the Greek, was filmed in our back yard; Stavro beach.

Visit the location where Anthony Quinn danced as Alexi Zorba and see the beautiful turquoise, lagoon-like beach.

If you like the outdoors and hiking, I can tell you where to take the best selfie of your entire trip. Cave Lera. Just above the charming beach on the distinctive mountain, you can see the shallow cave on the top. It is a steep hike but worth the climb.

The area has wonderful restaurants as well and a big playground for kids.

32. A VIEW FROM THE TOP (ROSA NERA)

A panoramic and undisturbed view of the old harbor and lighthouse is what you get from Rosa Nera; named after the rebellious youth organization that have made their permanent home in one of the buildings there.

If you search for pictures of Chania harbor, you will see them all taken either by drone, or a view from the top. This is the location to take the best selfie or panoramic picture.

To get to it, the easiest way is up the stairs next to the exhibition center (KAM), which is located in the street Michail Afentoulief. Easier yet is to use Pallas bar-restaurant as a guiding point (the street in question is on its right, opposite of the water). Once up the steps, walk to the right, through the iron gates and there! Bam! The view.

33. APTERA FORTRESS

Aptera is the general area and village there where you can have amazing an lunch and visit the archaeological site and ancient amphitheater.

What is most worth seeing to me though, is the view from the Koule (the fortress). This historic building has stood on the top of the mountain since 1866, after the Cretan revolution and was built by a Turk named Husein Avni.

>TOURIST

You cannot enter the actual Castillo but you can see Souda golf, Chania city and what I call the Big Blue.

It was named Aptera after the word 'wingless' which refers to the myth of the Sirens, they lost their wings in a competition against the muses of Crete and turned themselves in stone in the middle of the sea, which you can see from there.

34. TAKE CRETAN DANCE LESSONS

Crete, just like many islands in Greece, is proud of the culture and traditions. Nothing is more traditional than Cretan dances. You can find dance studios all over town but if you are not comfortable with classes you can always find some food fest where you can test your skills. The locals are very hospitable and would gladly help you to understand how it's done.

The most important dances in Crete are: Sirtos, Maleviziotis, Pedozali and Sousta. For anyone new to it, it is easier to learn Sigano (slow) Pedozali and Sirto.

The music that accompanies these seemingly difficult dances is usually made by two instruments:

the Lyra (a three-string instrument that sounds like the violin), and the Laouto an eight sting instrument.

Try it out, it's fun and you will get the real feeling of Crete.

35. SPLANTZIA SQUARE (1821)

In the heart of the center Splantzia square, also known as 1821 square to locals, is no ordinary locale. It is full of bloody history.

Splantzia was formally the main Ottoman district during Turkish rule. There are two churches in this square, the Venetian church of Saint Rocco which has been carefully preserved, and the church of Saint Nicholas.

Saint Nichola's church is very unique and has been standing for nearly 700 years. What makes this church so different is the fact that it is the only church in Greece that has both a bell tower and a minaret; it was turned into the Ottoman's central mosque.

The name was given to the square due to the hanging of the bishop of Kissamos on 19th of May 1821. The tree they were executed at still stands there, casting shade to the chilling location.

>TOURIST

You can find cafes and bars for a cold drink or beer, but it is worth the visit just for its history alone.

36. VISIT MILIA, A TRADITIONAL VILLAGE

When it comes to Chania, you never know what else you'll find; there is popular culture, history, traditions and something to suit each and every visitor.

If you are someone who likes quiet places where you can see the lives of the locals and learn from their traditions you must visit, and perhaps stay in, Milia. It is just an hour from the city center and worth the visit.

Milia is a village entirely built in stone where there is no electricity, Wi-Fi, cars or any other of your everyday amenities. The food is organic. The is wine locally made and even the water comes right from the creek.

I like visiting here to put my mind at ease, get in touch with nature and enjoy what is really important; good company. Whether it's great conversation over homemade food and organic wine or looking up at the natural light of the stars, it's all enjoyable when you have great people to share it with.

37. SEE THE OLDEST OLIVE TREE IN THE WORLD

In Ano Vouves just thirty minutes from the center of Chania off the main highway, you can find the oldest olive tree in the world.

No one has found the tree's exact age because its heart has been lost through the ages, but by studying the surrounding area the tree is presumably over three thousand years old.

What is astonishing is the fact that it still produces olive oil of the tsounati variety (a rare, local variety). In 1997 it was declared to a protected historic monument.

It is a really beautiful sight to see and fascinating to imagine how this tree has lasted through the ages.

A good idea is to combine the visit with a drive to Kolibari, the sea-front village.

>TOURIST

38. VISIT ELEFTHERIOS VENIZELOS' HOUSE

Eleftherios Venizelos has been one of the most influential politicians not only of Crete but of Greece as well. He was the one who united Crete and Greece in order to protect it from danger.

He was elected prime minister of Greece seven times and fought for Crete's liberation from the Germans.

One of his houses was built in 1876 but not completed until 1880. It is located in the Chalepa area just 1.4km from the center and a very interesting place to stop.

The house has been preserved till this day with its original character and furniture, so if political history is of interest, you should absolutely visit.

39. HAVE COFFEE IN 'KIPOS' HISTORIC CAFE

This cafe is within the biggest gardens in Chania and has operated since its creation in 1870.

Inside the cafe you can go through a photograph tour and learn all about its history.

'Kipos' cafe is also known not only for its highly trained servers, but also for its fresh delicious waffles.

I enjoy sipping on a hot chocolate there in the prestigious neo-classic, and well preserved dance hall.

There is great space provided for children to run around, a playground, a clock tower and a theater where you can watch black and white movies during the summer.

40. HORSEBACK IN DERE

Drive through villages of green and wildlife just a half hour from Chania and you can the 200 acre estate that is used as a horseback riding center. First opened in 1993, it has gained a reputation as a center that really cares for the horses, which you can see for yourselves as they set them free at the end of the day to run.

The estate offers four scenic rides suitable for both the experienced and the rookie.

Tour options:

- 1 hour tour up the mountain and extraordinary views of Chania city and surrounding isles.

\>TOURIST

- 2 hour tour across the mountain-tops with visit to a monastery near Kolibari.
- 3 hour tour through Limni village and stop in Dere picturesque village.
- 3 hour tour across the mountain-tops and ride on the beach of Tavroniti.

The estate operates on reservations alone.

*"A nation's culture resides
In the heart and the soul of its
people..."*

Mahatma Gandhi

41. 'AGROTIKOS AUGOUSTOS'

Would you like try local products from all over Crete without even getting in your car?

Every year at the end of August the city organizes a huge agriculture market, where producers and farmers can advertise their products. We call it 'Agrotikos Augoustos' which mean 'Agricultural August', and it has taken place in the 1866 square in the center of the city for the past three years.

You can try everything. That means, cheese, raki, honey, olive oil, rusks, wine and many more local goods.

Usually on the last day of this festival you can listen to live bands as well and watch traditional dances.

This is a fantastic way to get a taste of the culture, not just of Chania, but of the entire island.

42. ATTEND A FOOD – DRINK FESTIVAL

Summer in Crete is an endless party and there is always something to do or see and is usually a good time to visit. In autumn though, what is very common in Crete (yet tourists rarely seem to know it) are the food fests; such as the grape festival on the 2nd of September, the sardine festival on the 4th of September and some as late as the raki festival in the middle to end of October.

In these festivals the best approach is to go early and get a seat. Usually you pay a small entrance fee, which includes one carafe of wine or beer, and one or two dishes per paying visitor. It all depends on the type of festival you attend.

>TOURIST

You can also dance fearlessly with the locals and have a cuppa (responsibly) which they will surely offer.

The best of these events usually happen in small mountain villages such as: Vamos, Vrisses, Kolibari or to sum it up, anywhere with a church.

43. SEITAN LIMANIA

Get your hiking shoes on for this one, as it can become very slippery getting to this "hidden beach" which is no longer "hidden".

The name is of Turkish origin, and means 'Cursed Ports'. It was given to the beach – cove for two reasons.

One reason is because of its currents and secondly, because the Greeks would hide and attack unsuspecting invaders from within the cove and sink their enemy's ships.

The beach has become very popular but seeing as the beach is only two minutes from my house, I had to write about it. It is located just ten minutes from the airport, up and behind the mountain known as Skloka.

A few tips to keep in mind: 1. Go very early, 07:00 am if possible, or parking may be impossible and even dangerous. 2. Drive carefully and slowly. 3. Get plenty of water and forget cell reception, there is none.

44. DINE AT PALLAS ROOFTOP

One of the most innovative and fresh restaurants in town is known for its distinctive dishes, flavor filled cocktails and exquisite selection of wines.

Pallas restaurant has only improved with time from when it first opened its doors in late 90's, and only now are they re-opening the roof-garden to the public once again, years later.

Up on the roof-garden you can enjoy an intense culinary experience paired with a cold bottle of fine wine, and a view that will never grow old.

The funk and electro-soul tunes add their touch to an unforgettable evening.

Just remember to call for a reservation as it is always in high demand due to its views of the lighthouse.

>TOURIST

45. LOUTRAKI BEACH

I call it the beach of Chania's Elite; a gorgeous location that has only been revitalized in the past ten years to its current state, just ten minutes from the airport.

The water is deepest blue and rather cold at times, but what I like about the place is that there is grass instead of the usual sand that sticks in between your toes.

What is amazing also is that you can swim in the unforgettable waters and hear the music coming from the bar at the same time. It really brightens your day and is a great way to relax.

This beach is less known by tourists and more popular with the locals. The beach also offers water games for kids and adults so it's a great place to take the whole family.

46. BIKE THROUGH THERISSO GORGE

Therisso is a village of a historical value to Crete because of the revolution and uprising in 1905.

Beyond the historical importance though, it is a beautiful village to visit. I recommend you gear up with good hiking boots or bicycle though if you're intending to go.

This gorge is only 16km from Chania and it is worth hiking or riding through it. It is the only way to see and experience the scenery fully.

In Theriso village you can have a local lunch and most restaurants have playgrounds for kids and very good Rako-melo.

If you decide you want to make a day of it, my suggestion is to also visit the historical village of Panagia.

Alternatively, if you don't fancy a walk or bike ride you can drive, just beware of the tiny roads.

>TOURIST

47. VISIT THE BOTANICAL PARK AND GARDENS

Revived and restored the Botanical Park can be found in the village Fourne just 20km from Chania; on previously destroyed land from a large fire in 2003.

This is an ecological haven and a place where you can find not only rare Cretan herbs but plants, trees and fruit from all around the world. It is the only Botanical Park with three different climate type floras.

Take a two hour stroll down to see the lake, the wild Cretan animals and end the day with a taste of genuine Crete in the attached restaurant. It has received numerous awards and while there you where you can admire the views of the pure and green surroundings.

The restaurant and gardens are open from 09:00 am to sundown in the summer. Make sure to call in advance to avoid disappointment if you want to visit after October.

48. WALK TO THE LIGHTHOUSE

Sometimes we forget about the simple beauties our town possesses, and many may have never visited this iconic 500 year old monument.

As a symbol of Chania, it has stood in its current form since 1839. The Egyptians originally restored it, when Crete was given to them as gift of war from the Turks. I enjoy walking to it during sun set with an Ice-Cream in my hand. It never grows old.

It is a great spot to observe the sea, and being local to the city means this is a perfect place for a short excursion. So simple but so delightful.

49. DEVOUR A SFAKIANI PITTA

Sfakiani pitta originated from Chora Sfakion, south of Chania and it is a dessert that gets you addicted in just a few bites. If you want to eat like a local, I cannot recommend this enough.

>TOURIST

The pitta itself is made up of a thin dough which is then stuffed with local, soft cheese (Myzithra – something you must try in the Cretan salad), topped with local fresh thyme-honey. Sometimes they add pine nuts too.

Make sure you try this, it is a signature dish of Chania and it can be found literally everywhere.

50. SABBIONARA VIEWS

Chania city, also known as Canea in Venetian times, was protected all the way around with fortifications. Sabbionara is the last gate to still stand and to this day it bares the emblem of San Marco of Venice.

It is found in the neighborhood the Turks named "Koum Kapi" which means 'Gate of the Sand'. You can walk right up to it and appreciate the views of both sides of the harbor, and a spectacular sunset if you're there at the end of the day.

It is advisable to go before dark though.

You can also have coffee, wine or a snack in the historical building next to it, the Arsenal. This building has been used for the making of ships since ancient times.

\>TOURIST

TOP REASONS TO BOOK THIS TRIP

- **Beaches**: All beaches in Chania are magnificent. You want gold sand? You've got it! You want to hike to it and witness unforgettable sights? You've got it! We've got it all. To the locals however, the best beaches are found in the South of Chania.

- **Food**: The food is always fresh and traditional. You can choose from seafood, fresh fish and vegetable stews, to local, delicious meats. There's something for everyone.

- **Island Culture**: A rich heritage of tradition, and a proud one at that. The people are friendly and hospitable, so much so you will wish you never have to leave.

>TOURIST

Bonus Book

50 THINGS TO KNOW ABOUT PACKING LIGHT FOR TRAVEL

Pack the Right Way Every Time

Author: Manidipa Bhattacharyya

First Published in 2015 by Dr. Lisa Rusczyk. Copyright 2015. All Rights Reserved. No part of this publication may be reproduced, including scanning and photocopying, or distributed in any form or by any means, electronic or mechanical, or stored in a database or retrieval system without prior written permission from the publisher.

Disclaimer: The publisher has put forth an effort in preparing and arranging this book. The information provided herein by the author is provided "as is". Use this information at your own risk. The publisher is not a licensed doctor. Consult your doctor before engaging in any medical activities. The publisher and author disclaim any liabilities for any loss of profit or commercial or personal damages resulting from the information contained in this book.

Edited by Melanie Howthorne

Introduction

He who would travel happily
must travel light.

-Antoine de Saint-Exupéry

Travel takes you to different places from seas and mountains to deserts and much more. In your travels you get to interact with different people and their cultures. You will, however, enjoy the sights and interact positively with these new people even more, if you are travelling light.

When you travel light your mind can be free from worry about your belongings. You do not have to spend precious vacation time waiting for your luggage to arrive after a long flight. There is be no chance of your bags going missing and the best part is that you need not pay a fee for checked baggage.

People who have mastered this art of packing light will root for you to take only one carry-on, wherever you go. However, many people can find it really hard to pack light. More so if you are travelling with children. Differentiating between "must have" and "just in case" items is the starting point. There will be ample shopping avenues at your destination which are just waiting to be explored.

This book will show you 'packing' in a new 'light' – pun intended – and help you to embrace light packing practices for all of your future travels.

Off to packing!

Dedication

I dedicate this book to all the travel buffs that I know, who have given me great insights into the contents of their backpacks.

About The Author

Manidipa Bhattacharyya is a creative writer and editor, with an education in English literature and Linguistics. After working in the IT industry for seven long years she decided to call it quits and follow her heart instead. Manidipa has been ghost writing, editing, proof reading and doing secondary research services for many story tellers and article writers for about three years. She stays in Kolkata, India with her husband and a busy two year old. In her own time Manidipa enjoys travelling, photography and writing flash fiction.

Manidipa believes in travelling light and never carries anything that she couldn't haul herself on a trip. However, travelling with her child changed the scenario. She seemed to carry the entire world with her for the baby on the first two trips. But good sense prevailed and she is again working her way to becoming a light traveler, this time with a kid.

The Right Travel Gear

1. Choose Your Travel Gear Carefully

While selecting your travel gear, pick items that are light weight, durable and most importantly, easy to carry. There are cases with wheels so you can drag them along – these are usually on the heavy side because of the trolley. Alternatively a backpack that you can carry comfortably on your back, or even a duffel bag that you can carry easily by hand or sling across your body are also great options. Whatever you choose, one thing to keep in mind is that the luggage itself should not weigh a ton, this will give you the flexibility to bring along one extra pair of shoes if you so desire.

2. Carry The Minimum Number Of Bags

Selecting light weight luggage is not everything. You need to restrict the number of bags you carry as well. One carry-on size bag is ideal for light travel. Most carriers allow one cabin baggage plus one purse, handbag or camera bag as long as it slides under the seat in front. So technically, you can carry two items of luggage without checking them in.

3. Pack One Extra Bag

>TOURIST

Always pack one extra empty bag along with your essential items. This could be a very light weight duffel bag or even a sturdy tote bag which takes up minimal space. In the event that you end up buying a lot of souvenirs, you already have a handy bag to stuff all that into and do not have to spend time hunting for an appropriate bag.

> *I'm very strict with my packing and have everything in its right place. I never change a rule. I hardly use anything in the hotel room. I wheel my own wardrobe in and that's it.*
>
> Charlie Watts

Clothes & Accessories

4. Plan Ahead

Figure out in advance what you plan to do on your trip. That will help you to pick that one dress you need for the occasion. If you are going to attend a wedding then you have to carry formal wear. If not, you can ditch the gown for something lighter that will be comfortable during long walks or on the beach.

5. Wear That Jacket

Remember that wearing items will not add extra luggage for your air travel. So wear that bulky jacket that you plan to carry for your trip. This saves space and can also help keep you warm during the chilly flight.

6. Mix and Match

Carry clothes that can be interchangeably used to reinvent your look. Find one top that goes well with a couple of pairs of pants or skirts. Use tops, shirts and jackets wisely along with other accessories like a scarf or a stole to create a new look.

7. Choose Your Fabric Wisely

Stuffing clothes in cramped bags definitely takes its toll which results in wrinkles. It is best to carry wrinkle free, synthetic clothes or merino tops. This will eliminate the need for that small iron you usually bring along.

8. Ditch Clothes Pack Underwear

Pack more underwear and socks. These are the things that will give you a fresh feel even if you do not get a chance to wear fresh clothes. Moreover these are easy to wash and can be dried inside the hotel room itself.

9. Choose Dark Over Light

While picking your clothes choose dark coloured ones. They are easy to colour coordinate and can last longer before needing a wash. Accidental food spills and dirt from the road are less visible on darker clothes.

10. Wear Your Jeans

Take only one pair of Jeans with you, which you should wear on the flight. Remember to pick a pair that can be worn for sightseeing trips and is equally eloquent for dinner. You can add variety by adding light weight cargoes and chinos.

11. Carry Smart Accessories

The right accessory can give you a fresh look even with the same old dress. An intelligent neck-piece, a couple of bright scarves, stoles or a sarong can be used in a number of ways to add variety to your clothing. These light weight beauties can double up as a nursing cover, a light blanket, beach wear, a modesty cover for visiting places of worship, and also makes for an enthralling game of peek-a-boo.

12. Learn To Fold Your Garments

Seasoned travellers all swear by rolling their clothes for compact and wrinkle free packing. Bundle packing, where you roll the clothes around a central object as if tying it up, is also a popular method of compact and wrinkle free packing. Stacking folded clothes one on top of another is a big no-no as it makes creases extreme and they are difficult to get rid of without ironing.

13. Wash Your Dirty Laundry

One of the ways to avoid carrying loads of clothes is to wash the clothes you carry. At some places you might get to use the laundry services or a Laundromat but if you are in a pinch, best solution is to wash them yourself. If that is the plan then carrying quick drying clothes is highly recommended, which most often also happen to be the wrinkle free variety.

14. Leave Those Towels Behind

Regular towels take up a lot of space, are heavy and take ages to dry out. If you are staying at hotels they will provide you with towels anyway. If you are travelling to a remote place, where the availability of towels look doubtful, carry a light weight travel towel of viscose material to do the job.

15. Use A Compression Bag

Compression bags are getting lots of recommendation now days from regular travellers. These are useful for saving space in your luggage when you have to pack bulky dresses. While packing for the return trip, get help from the hotel staff to arrange a vacuum cleaner.

Footwear

16. Put On Your Hiking Boots

If you have plans to go hiking or trekking during your trip, you will need those bulky hiking boots. The best way to carry them is to wear them on flight to save space and luggage weight. You can remove the boots once inside and be comfortable in your socks.

17. Picking The Right Shoes

Shoes are often the bulkiest items, along with being the dainty if you are a female. They need care and take up a lot of space in your luggage. It is advisable therefore to pick shoes very carefully. If you plan to do a lot of walking and site seeing, then wearing a pair of comfortable walking shoes are a must. For more formal occasions you can carry durable, light weight flats which will not take up much space.

18. Stuff Shoes

If you happen to pack a pair of shoes, ensure you utilize their hollow insides. Tuck small items like rolled up socks or belts to save space. They will also be easy to find.

Toiletries
19. Stashing Toiletries

Carry only absolute necessities. Airline rules dictate that for one carry-on bag, liquids and gels must be in 3.4 ounce (100ml) bottles or less, and must be packed in a one quart zip-lock bag. If you are planning to stay in a hotel, the basic things will be provided for you. It's best is to buy the rest from the local market at your destination.

20. Take Along Tampons

Tampons are a hard to find item in a lot of countries. Figure out how many you need and pack accordingly. For longer stays you can buy them online and have them delivered to where you are staying.

21. Get Pampered Before You Travel

Some avid travellers suggest getting a pedicure and manicure just the day before travelling. This not only gives you a well kept look, you also save the trouble of packing nail polish. Remember, every little bit of weight reduced adds up.

Electronics
22. Lugging Along Electronics

Electronics have a large role to play in our lives today. Most of us cannot imagine our lives away from our phones, laptops or tablets. However while travelling, one must consider the amount of weight these electronics add to our luggage. Thankfully smart phones come along with all the essentials tools like a camera, email access, picture editing tools and more. They are smart to the point of eliminating the need to carry multiple gadgets. Choose a smart phone that suits all your requirements and travel with the world in your palms or pocket.

23. Reduce the Number of Chargers

If you do travel with multiple electronic devices, you will have to bear the additional burden of carrying all their chargers too. Check if a single charger can be used for multiple devices. You might also consider investing in a pocket charger. These small devices support multiple devices while keeping you charged on the go.

24. Travel Friendly Apps

Along with smart phones come numerous apps, which are immensely helpful in our travels. You name it and you have an app for it at hand – take pictures, sharing with friends and family, torch to light dark roads, maps, checking flight/train times, find hotels and many other things. Use these smart alternatives to traditional items like books to eliminate weight and save space.

I get ideas about what's essential when packing my suitcase.

-Diane von Furstenberg

Travelling With Kids

25. Bring Along the Stroller

Kids might enjoy walking for a while but they soon tire out and a stroller is the just the right thing for them to rest in while you continue your tour. Strollers also double duty as a luggage carrier and shopping bag holder. Remember to pick a light weight, easy to handle brand of stroller. Better yet, find out in advance if you can rent a stroller at your destination.

26. Bring Only Enough Diapers for Your Trip

Diapers take up a lot of space and add to the weight of your luggage. Therefore it is advisable to carry just enough diapers to last through the trip and a few for afterwards, till you buy fresh stock at your destination. Unless of course you are travelling to a really remote area, in which case you have no choice but to carry the load. Otherwise diapers are something you will find pretty easily.

27. Take Only A Couple Of Toys

Children are easily attracted by new things in their environment. While travelling they will find numerous 'new' objects to scrutinize and play with. Packing just one favorite toy is enough, or if there is no favorite toy leave out all of them in favor of stories or imaginary games.

28. Carry Kid Friendly Snacks

Create a small snack counter in your bag to store away quick bites for those sudden hunger pangs. Depending on the child's age this could include chocolates, raisins, dry fruits, granola bars or biscuits. Also keep a bottle of water handy for your little one. These things do not add much weight and can be adjusted in a handbag or knapsack.

29. Games to Carry

Create some travel specific, imaginary games if you have slightly grown up children, like spot the attractions. Keep a coloring book and colors handy for in-flight or hotel time. Apps on your smart phone can keep the children engaged with cartoons and story books. Older children are often entertained by games

>TOURIST

available on phones or tablets. This cuts the weight of luggage down while keeping the kids entertained.

30. Let the Kids Carry Their Load

A good thing is to start early sharing of responsibilities. Let your child pick a bag of his or her choice and pack it themselves. Keep tabs on what they are stuffing in their bags by asking if they will be using that item on the trip. It could start out being just an entertainment bag initially but with growing years they will learn to sort the useful from the superfluous. Children as little as four can maneuver a small trolley suitcase like a pro- their experience in pull along toys credit. If you are worried that you may be pulling it for them, you may want to start with a backpack.

31. Decide on Location for Children to Sleep

While on a trip you might not always get a crib at your destination, and carrying one will make life all the more difficult. Instead call ahead to see if there are any cribs or roll out beds for children. You may even put blankets on the floor. Weave them a story about camping and they will gladly sleep without any trouble.

32. Get Baby Products Delivered At Your Destination

If you are absolutely paranoid about not getting your favourite variety of diaper or brand of baby food, check out online stores like amazon.com for services in your destination city. You can buy things online ahead of your travel and get them delivered to your hotel upon arrival.

33. Feeding Needs Of Your Infants

If you are travelling with a breastfed infant, you save the trouble of carrying bottles and bottle sanitization kits. For special food, or medications, you may need to call ahead to make sure you have a refrigerator where you are staying.

34. Feeding Needs of Your Toddler

With the progression from infancy to toddler, their dietary requirements too evolve. You will have to pack some snacks for travelling time. Fresh fruits and vegetables can be purchased at your destination. Most of the cities you travel to in whichever part of the world, will have baby food products and formulas, available at the local drug-store or the supermarket.

>TOURIST

35. Picking Clothes for Your Baby

Contrary to popular belief, babies can do without many changes of clothes. At the most pack 2 outfits per day. Pack mix and match type clothes for your little one as well. Pick things which are comfortable to wear and quick to dry.

36. Selecting Shoes for Your Baby

Like outfits, kids can make do with two pairs of comfortable shoes. If you can get some water resistant shoes it will be best. To expedite drying wet shoes, you can stuff newspaper in them then wrap them with newspaper and leave them to dry overnight.

37. Keep One Change of Clothes Handy

Travelling with kids can be tricky. Keep a change of clothes for the kids and mum handy in your purse or tote bag. This takes a bit of space in your hand luggage but comes extremely handy in case there are any accidents or spills.

38. Leave Behind Baby

Accessories

Baby accessories like their bed, bath tub, car seat, crib etc. should be left at home. Many hotels provide a crib on request, while car seats can be borrowed from friends or rented. Babies can be given a bath in the hotel sink or even in the adult bath tub with a little bit of water. If you bring a few bath toys, they can be used in the bath, pool, and out of water. They can also be sanitized easily in the sink.

39. Carry a Small Load Of Plastic Bags

With children around there are chances of a number of soiled clothes and diapers. These plastic bags help to sort the dirt from the clean inside your big bag. These are very light weight and come in handy to other carry stuff as well at times.

Pack with a Purpose

40. Packing for Business Trips

One neutral-colored suit should suffice. It can be paired with different shirts, ties and accessories for different occasions. One pair of black suit pants could be worn with a matching jacket for the office or with a snazzy top for dinner.

41. Packing for A Cruise

Most cruises have formal dinners, and that formal dress usually takes up a lot of space. However you might find a tuxedo to rent. For women, a short black dress with multiple accessory options will do the trick.

42. Packing for A Long Trip Over Different Climates

The secret packing mantra for travel over multiple climates is layering. Layering traps air around your body creating insulation against the cold. The same light t-shirt that is comfortable in a warmer climate can be the innermost layer in a colder climate.

Reduce Some More Weight

43. Leave Precious Things At Home

Things that you would hate to lose or get damaged leave them at home. Precious jewelry, expensive gadgets or dresses, could be anything. You will not require these on your trip. Leave them at home and spare the load on your mind.

44. Send Souvenirs by Mail

If you have spent all your money on purchasing souvenirs, carrying them back in the same bag that you brought along would be difficult. Either pack everything in another bag and check it in the airport or get everything shipped to your home. Use an international carrier for a secure transit, but this could be more expensive than the checking fees at the airport.

45. Avoid Carrying Books

Books equal to weight. There are many reading apps which you can download on your smart phone or tab. Plus there are gadgets like Kindle and Nook that are thinner and lighter alternatives to your regular book.

Check, Get, Set, Check Again

46. Strategize Before Packing

Create a travel list and prepare all that you think you need to carry along. Keep everything on your bed or floor before packing and then think through once again – do I really need that? Any item that meets this question can be avoided. Remove whatever you don't really need and pack the rest.

>TOURIST

47. Test Your Luggage

Once you have fully packed for the trip take a test trip with your luggage. Take your bags and go to town for window shopping for an hour. If you enjoy your hour long trip it is good to go, if not, go home and reduce the load some more. Repeat this test till you hit the right weight.

48. Add a Roll Of Duct Tape

You might wonder why, when this book has been talking about reducing stuff, we're suddenly asking you to pack something totally unusual. This is because when you have limited supplies, duct tape is immensely helpful for small repairs – a broken bag, leaking zip-lock bag, broken sunglasses, you name it and duct tape can fix it, temporarily.

49. List of Essential Items

Even though the emphasis is on packing light, there are things which have to be carried for any trip. Here is our list of essentials:

- Passport/Visa or any other ID
- Any other paper work that might be required on a trip like permits, hotel reservation confirmations etc.

- Medicines – all your prescription medicines and emergency kit, especially if you are travelling with children

- Medical or vaccination records

- Money in foreign currency if travelling to a different country

- Tickets- Email or Message them to your phone

50. Make the Most of Your Trip

Wherever you are going, whatever you hope to do we encourage you to embrace it whole-heartedly. Take in the scenery, the culture and above all, enjoy your time away from home.

On a long journey even a straw weighs heavy.

-Spanish Proverb

>TOURIST

Packing and Planning Tips

A Week before Leaving

- Arrange for someone to take care of pets and water plants
- •Stop mail and newspaper
- Notify Credit Card companies where you are going.
- Change your thermostat settings
- Car inspected, oil is changed, and tires have the correct pressure.
- Passports and id is up to date.
- Pay bills.
- Copy important items and download travel Apps.
- Start collecting small bills for tips

Right Before Leaving

- Clean out refrigerator.
- Empty garbage cans.
- Lock windows.
- Make sure you have the right ID with you.
- Bring cash for tips.
- Remember travel documents.
- Lock door behind you.
- Remember wallet.
- Unplug items in house and pack chargers.

>TOURIST

Read other Greater Than a Tourist Books

Greater Than a Tourist San Miguel de Allende Guanajuato Mexico: 50 Travel Tips from a Local by Tom Peterson

Greater Than a Tourist – Lake George Area New York USA: 50 Travel Tips from a Local by Janine Hirschklau

Greater Than a Tourist – Monterey California United States: 50 Travel Tips from a Local by Katie Begley

Greater Than a Tourist – Chanai Crete Greece: 50 Travel Tips from a Local by Dimitra Papagrigoraki

Greater Than a Tourist – The Garden Route Western Cape Province South Africa: 50 Travel Tips from a Local by Li-Anne McGregor van Aardt

Greater Than a Tourist – Sevilla Andalusia Spain: 50 Travel Tips from a Local by Gabi Gazon

Greater Than a Tourist – Kota Bharu Kelantan Malaysia: 50 Travel Tips from a Local by Aditi Shukla

Children's Book: Charlie the Cavalier Travels the World by Lisa Rusczyk

> TOURIST

Visit Greater Than a Tourist for Free Travel Tips
http://GreaterThanATourist.com

Sign up for the Greater Than a Tourist Newsletter for discount days, new books, and travel information:
http://eepurl.com/cxspyf

Follow us on Facebook for tips, images, and ideas:
https://www.facebook.com/GreaterThanATourist

Follow us on Pinterest for travel tips and ideas:
http://pinterest.com/GreaterThanATourist

Follow us on Instagram for beautiful travel images:
http://Instagram.com/GreaterThanATourist

> TOURIST

Please leave your honest review of this book on Amazon and Goodreads. Please send your feedback to GreaterThanaTourist@gmail.com as we continue to improve the series. Thank you. We appreciate your positive and constructive feedback. Thank you.

>TOURIST

NOTES

Printed in Great Britain
by Amazon

75219522R00064